Gareth Stevens
PUBLISHING

Wildly Weird Weather

It's a Volcano Tornado!

By Rachael Morlock

Please visit our website, www.garethstevens.com. For a free color catalog of all our high-quality books, call toll free 1-800-542-2595 or fax 1-877-542-2596.

Cataloging-in-Publication Data

Names: Morlock, Rachael.
Title: It's a volcano tornado! / Rachael Morlock.
Description: New York : Gareth Stevens Publishing, 2024. | Series: Wildly weird weather | Includes glossary and index.
Identifiers: ISBN 9781538287910 (pbk.) | ISBN 9781538287927 (library bound) | ISBN 9781538287934 (ebook)
Subjects: LCSH: Volcanoes–Juvenile literature. | Volcanoes–Miscellanea–Juvenile literature. | Tornadoes–Juvenile literature.
Classification: LCC QE521.3 M646 2024 | DDC 363.34'95–dc23

First Edition

Published in 2024 by
Gareth Stevens Publishing
2544 Clinton St.
Buffalo, NY 14224

Designer: Corinne Eberwine
Editor: Theresa Emminizer

Photo credits: Cover (volcano), Romolo Tavani/Shutterstock.com; Cover (tornado), Romolo Tavani/Shutterstock.com; p. 5 Wead/Shutterstock.com; p. 6 (graphic) OSweetNature/Shutterstock.com; p. 9 Marco Ritzki/Shutterstock.com; p. 10 Oliver Spalt/Wikimedia.com; p. 13 Minerva Studio/Shutterstock.com; p. 14 U.S. Fish and Wildlife Service/Wikimedia.com; p. 17 Thorir Ingvarsson/Shutterstock.com; p. 18 Naeblys/Shutterstock.com; p. 21 Ragnar Th Sigurdsson/Alamy.com.

Printed in the United States of America

CPSIA compliance information: Batch #CS24GS: For further information contact Gareth Stevens, New York, New York at 1-800-542-2595.

CONTENTS

Words in the glossary appear in **bold** type the first time they are used in the text.

Tornado Meets Volcano

Imagine a sleeping volcano **erupting**. The ground rumbles. Clouds of ash and smoke fill the air. Glowing lava flows like a river. Dark clouds gather over the blazing volcano. Suddenly, a swirling tower appears. It rises from the earth up into the sky. It's a volcano tornado!

Volcanic eruptions are the most powerful force in nature. Eruptions at Mount Etna in Italy, shown here, shoot lava into the air. >

Some volcanic eruptions are so powerful that they create storms. Heat, steam, ash, and gases from the volcano mix with the **atmosphere**. When the conditions are right, they can form a kind of tornado.

What's a Volcano?

Earth is made up of layers. The top layer is Earth's crust. A layer of rock called the mantle lies below the crust. Liquid rock called magma is melted by Earth's super-hot core.

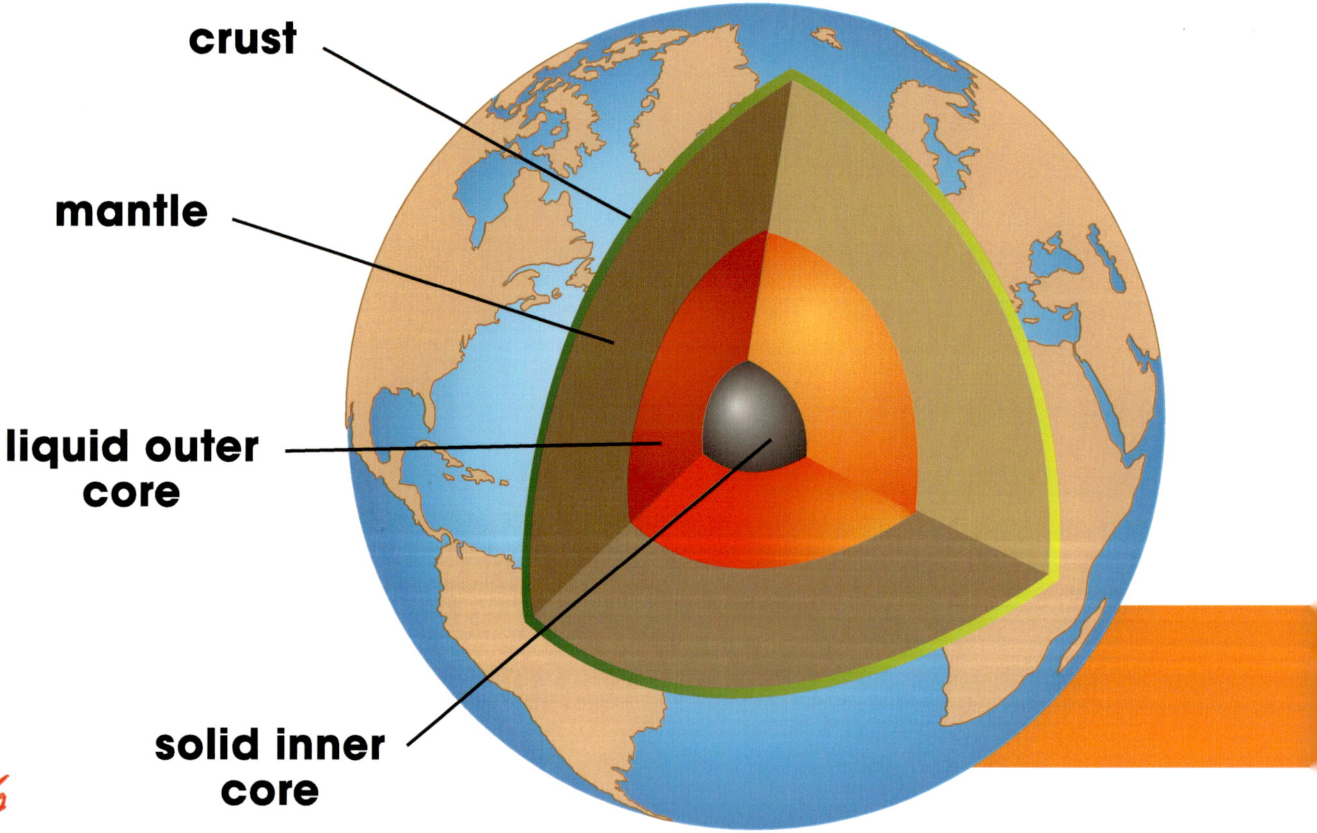

THAT'S A FACT!

A volcano can be active, which means it has erupted recently, or it can be dormant, which means it has not erupted in many years. Extinct volcanoes are not likely to erupt again.

Sometimes, magma and gases rise through the mantle and reach Earth's surface. A volcano is a vent, or crack, in Earth's crust. The name volcano also refers to the **landform** around the vent. An eruption occurs when hot magma and gases move up through the vent and out of the volcano.

The closer a layer of Earth is to the center, or core, of the planet, the hotter it is. Earth's inner core is as hot as the surface of the sun.

Volcanic Eruptions

Magma that erupts from a volcano is called lava. Lava can reach up to 2,000°F (1,093°C)! Gases from deep below Earth's surface also come out of a volcano during an eruption. Some volcanoes shoot hot gas, rocks, and ash in a deadly flow.

THAT'S A FACT!

About 1,350 volcanoes are active in countries around the world. Even more volcanoes are on the ocean floor. Underwater, or submarine, volcanoes can erupt and send hot steam and water flying!

Lava cools into rock and creates new landforms. Each eruption can change the shape of the volcano as rock and ash build up over time. Lava that hits the ocean can create new islands or underwater mountains.

Here, red-hot lava flows from a volcano in Iceland. Lava might quickly explode or slowly stream out of a volcano.

Stormy Weather

Volcanoes are so powerful that they can create their own weather. Some volcanoes send a big cloud of ash into the air. Tiny bits of ash swirl and bump into each other. They rub together and swap **electrons** through a force called **friction**. When there is enough friction in the ash cloud, lightning strikes!

Storms of rain, lightning, and thunder often take place above an eruption. This picture of volcanic lightning was captured at Mount Rinjani, Indonesia.

Ash can also collect water droplets. When this happens, a type of thundercloud can form above the ash. This special fire cloud can even cause rain!

THAT'S A FACT!

Most lightning happens early in a volcanic eruption before the bits of ash drift away from each other through the air. Usually, more ash means more lightning.

What's a Tornado?

A tornado is a spinning **column** of air that forms in a cloud and touches the ground. A tornado creates strong, fast wind as it twists in the air. It can move quickly, harm people, and destroy buildings and land.

THAT'S A FACT!

Tornadoes stir up winds that can move as fast as 300 miles (482.8 km) per hour! After a tornado touches the land, it travels at about 28 miles (45 km) per hour.

Most tornadoes happen during thunderstorms. Hot and cold air crash together and start **rotating** in a circle called a **vortex**. The vortex grows taller and becomes a spinning tower. Very hot air above a volcanic eruption can also cause a vortex to form.

The spinning tower of a tornado is called a funnel cloud. This funnel cloud has a cone shape. Water droplets in the funnel make the tornado ***visible.***

Tornado or Fire Whirl?

A true tornado forms in a cloud. It needs warm, humid air near the ground to mix with cool, dry air above. It also needs rotating wind. With the right conditions, it's possible for a volcanic storm to produce a true tornado.

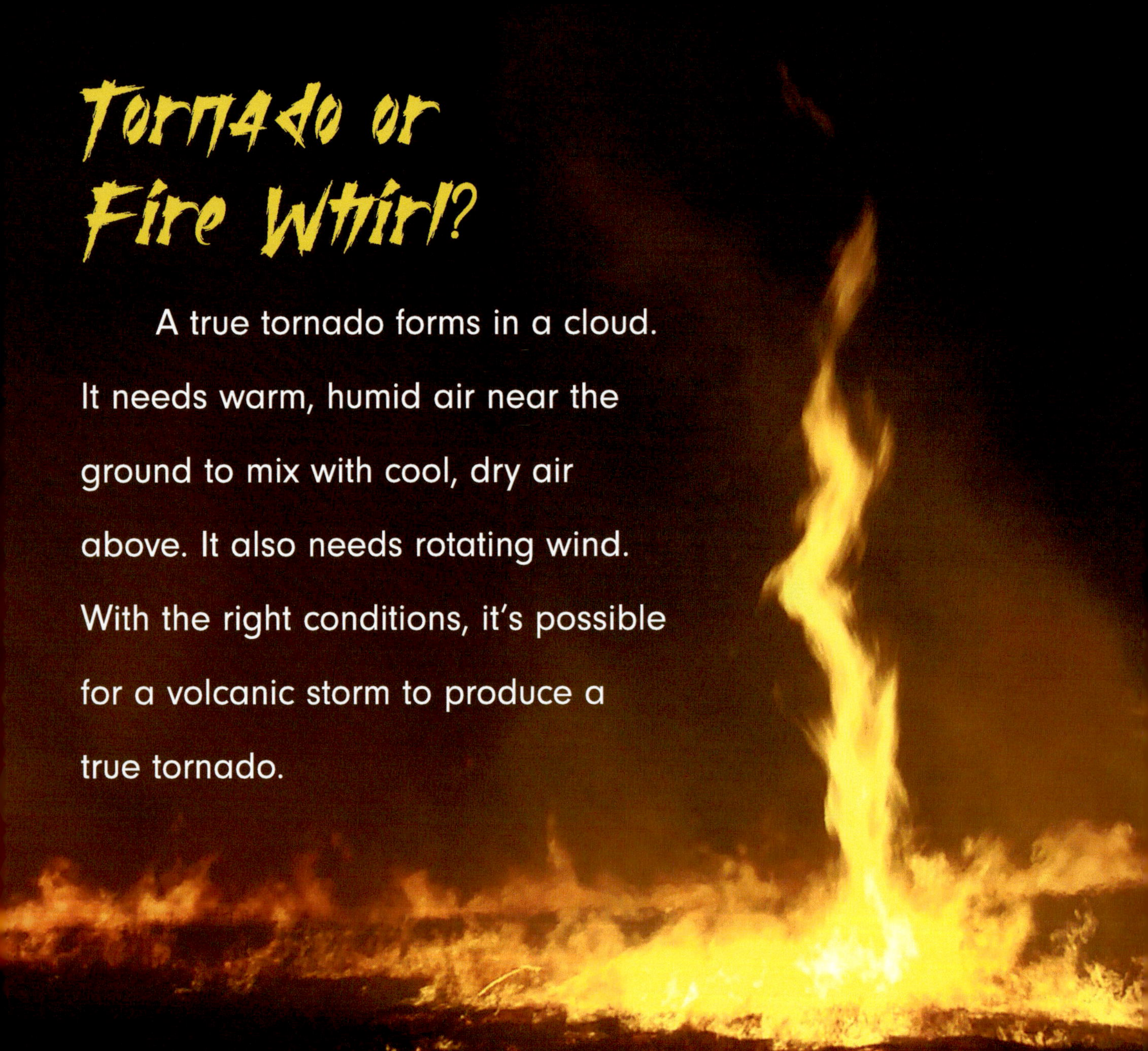

In this picture, hot air rising from a burning field forms a fire whirl.

However, it's more common for volcanoes to create other kinds of vortexes. These start down at the ground instead of up in a cloud. A fire whirl is one example. It looks like a small tornado made of flame.

THAT'S A FACT!

Volcanic fire whirls are similar to the fire tornadoes formed by wildfires. In 2018, the Carr fire in California created a huge fire tornado that reached 17,000 feet (5,182 m) into the sky.

Look Out for Lava Devils!

As lava flows, it heats the air above it. This hot air can create a version of a fire whirl called a lava devil. It's more like a "lavanado" than a tornado!

Lava devils begin when an **updraft** of hot air forms a vortex that picks up lava. As it spins, a lava devil sprays out lava and chunks of rock. Lava devils were seen in the 2018 eruption of Kilauea in Hawaii.

In 2021, the erupting Fagradalsfjall volcano in Iceland produced lava devils. The devils began swirling over the stream of lava and moved toward the lava fountain at the mouth of the volcano.

This model shows the eruption of a submarine volcano. Underwater eruptions can blast steam and water out of the ocean.

Ash and Water

Volcanic eruptions can also produce a type of mini tornado called a landspout. A landspout starts on the ground. It spins more slowly than a regular tornado. Instead of picking up lava and rocks, a volcanic landspout twirls ash in the air.

A kind of volcano tornado can form over water too. Lava from a volcano can flow into water and create steam. The hot steam swirls in a vortex that rises into the air. It carries water droplets with it.

Toxic Gases

Volcanoes can create whirling towers of fire, lava, ash, and water. They can also make funnels of **toxic** gases. In 2014, the Holuhraun volcano erupted in Iceland and created whirls of sulfur dioxide. The columns of gas rose 3,300 feet (1,005.8 m) into the air!

Scientists are still learning about the different ways volcanoes affect the weather around them. Studying wild events like fire whirls, lava devils, and landspouts will give scientists new ways to **classify** and explain volcano tornadoes.

The whirls of gas at the Holuhraun volcano were made of sulfur dioxide. When sulfur burns and mixes with oxygen, it causes air pollution and makes breathing difficult.

Glossary

atmosphere: The mixture of gases that surround a planet.

classify: To assign something to a category or class based on shared qualities.

column: A long, tall pole shape.

electron: A particle found in atoms that acts as a carrier of electricity in solids.

erupt: To burst forth.

friction: The force that slows motion between two objects touching each other.

landform: A natural feature on Earth's surface.

rotate: To turn around a fixed point.

toxic: Containing harmful substances.

updraft: An upward flow of air.

visible: Able to be seen.

vortex: A spinning mass of air or liquid that pulls substances into its center.

For More Information

Books

Berg, Shannon. *Hawaii Volcano of 2018.* Lake Elmo, MN: Focus Readers, 2020.

Jenkins, Steve. *Disasters by the Numbers: A Book of Infographics.* Boston, MA: Houghton Mifflin Harcourt, 2021.

Van Rose, Susanna. *Volcano and Earthquake.* New York, NY: DK Publishing, 2022.

Websites

Britannica Kids: Tornado
www.kids.britannica.com/kids/article/tornado/399626
This article explains what a tornado is and how it forms.

National Geographic
www.nationalgeographic.co.uk/video/tv/rare-tornadoes-on-hawaiis-kilauea-volcano
You can watch landspouts forming over Kilauea in this video from National Geographic.

Weather Wiz Kids: Volcanoes
www.weatherwizkids.com/?page_id=98
Find all the answers to your questions about volcanoes on this web page.

Publisher's note to educators and parents: Our editors have carefully reviewed these websites to ensure that they are suitable for students. Many websites change frequently, however, and we cannot guarantee that a site's future contents will continue to meet our high standards of quality and educational value. Be advised that students should be closely supervised whenever they access the internet.

Index